The rules of this book are few and simple: complete the most difficult challenges to get as many points as possible and become the WORLD CHAMPION.

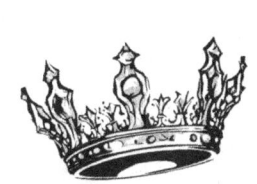 

Can you handle it?

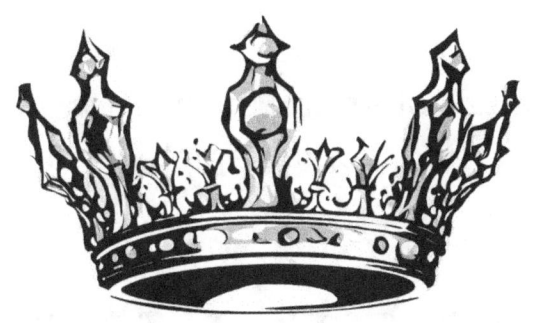

THE CHALLENGES:

-One line: 5 pts

-Black and white: 4 pts

-Never erase: 3 pts

-Less than 15 minutes: 2 pts

-Drawing completed: 1 pt

(You obtain the amount of points of the most difficult challenge that you complete)

GOOD LUCK

She loves anime

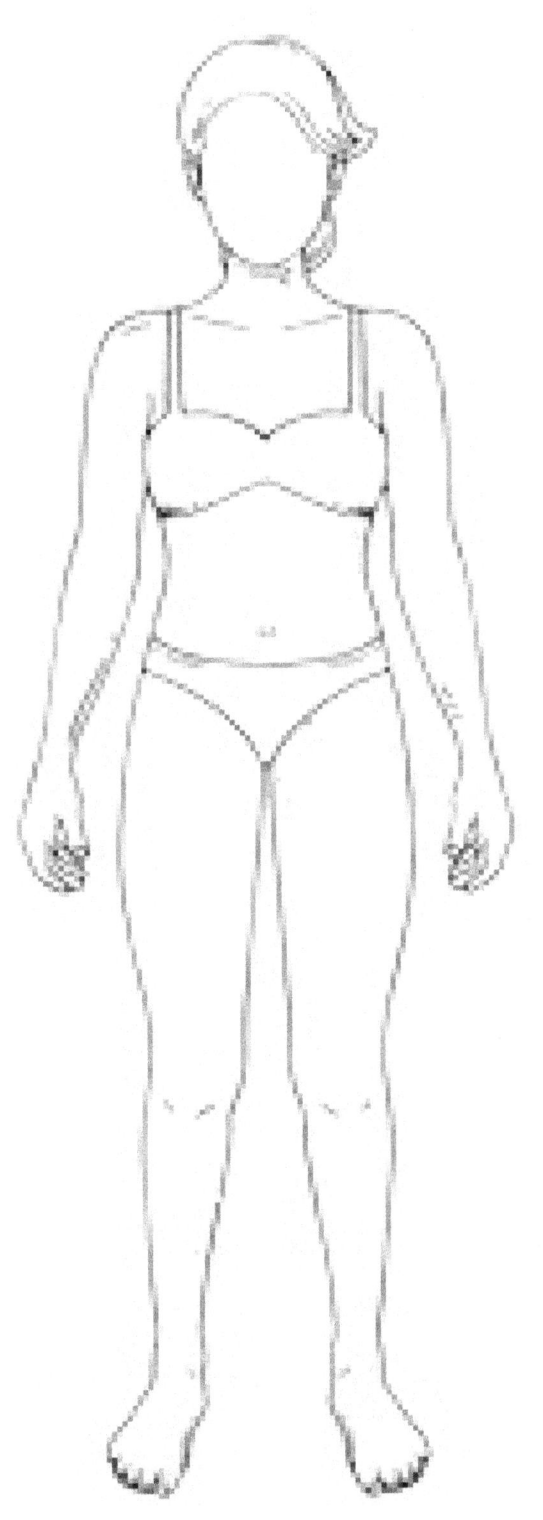

/5

She is your mother

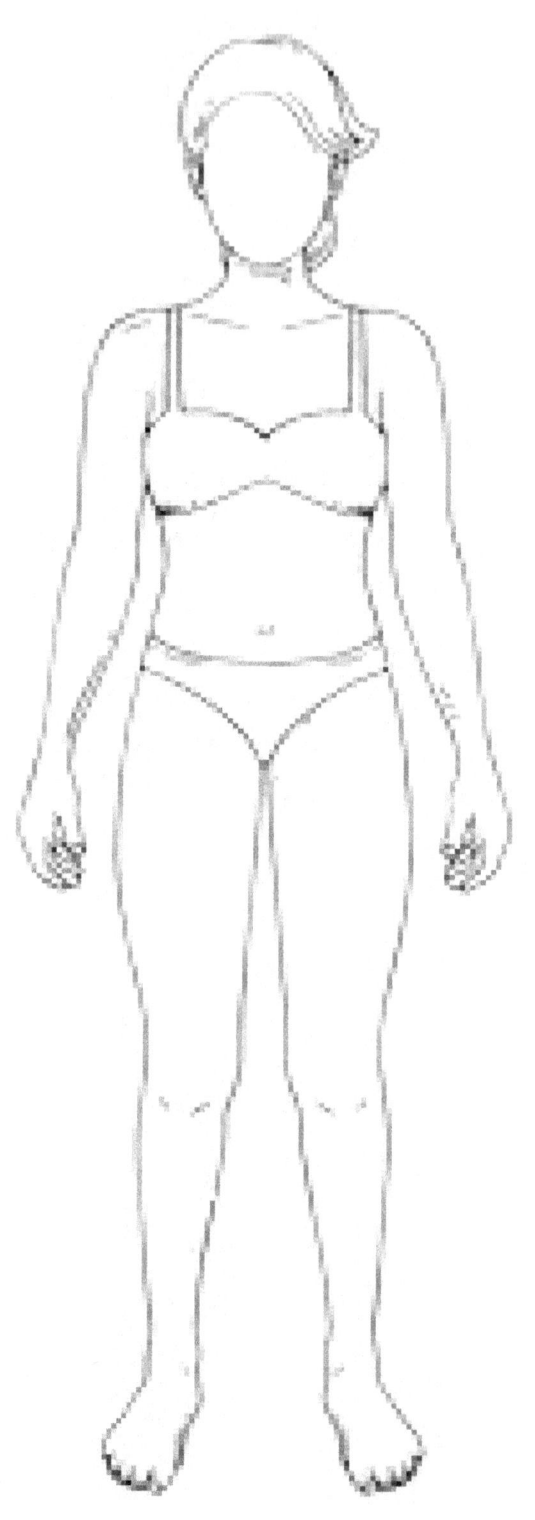

/5

She woke up with the wrong foot

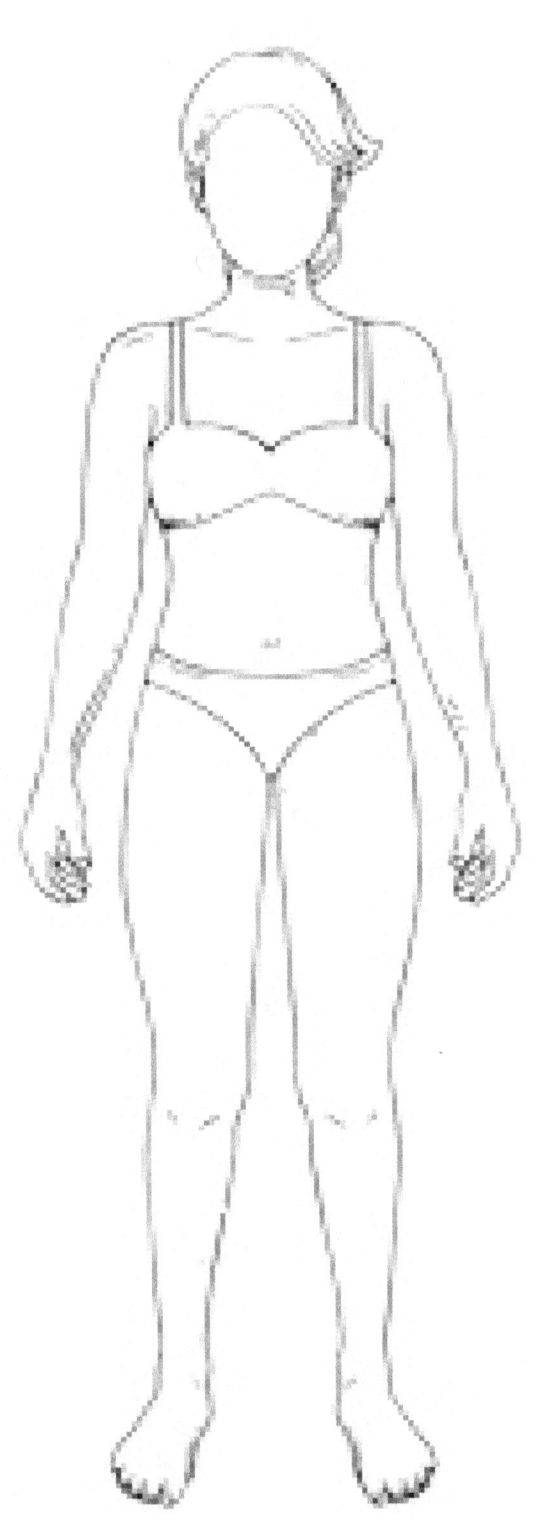

/5

She is a song-writer

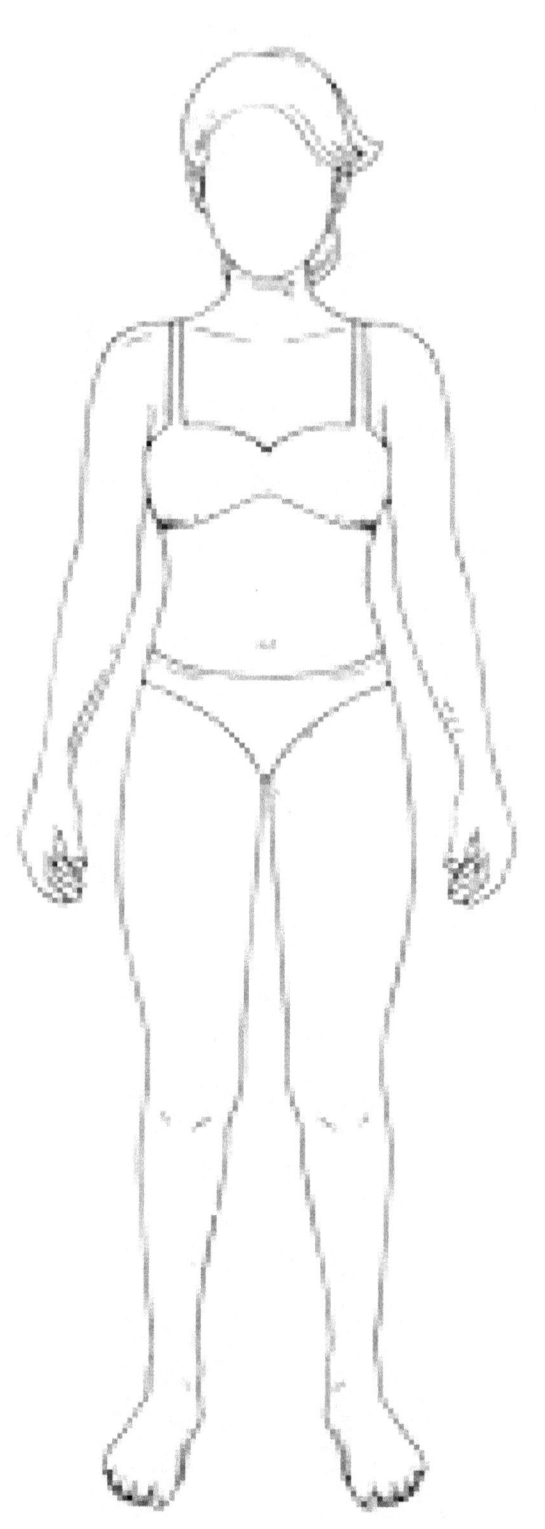

/5

She is about to go hiking

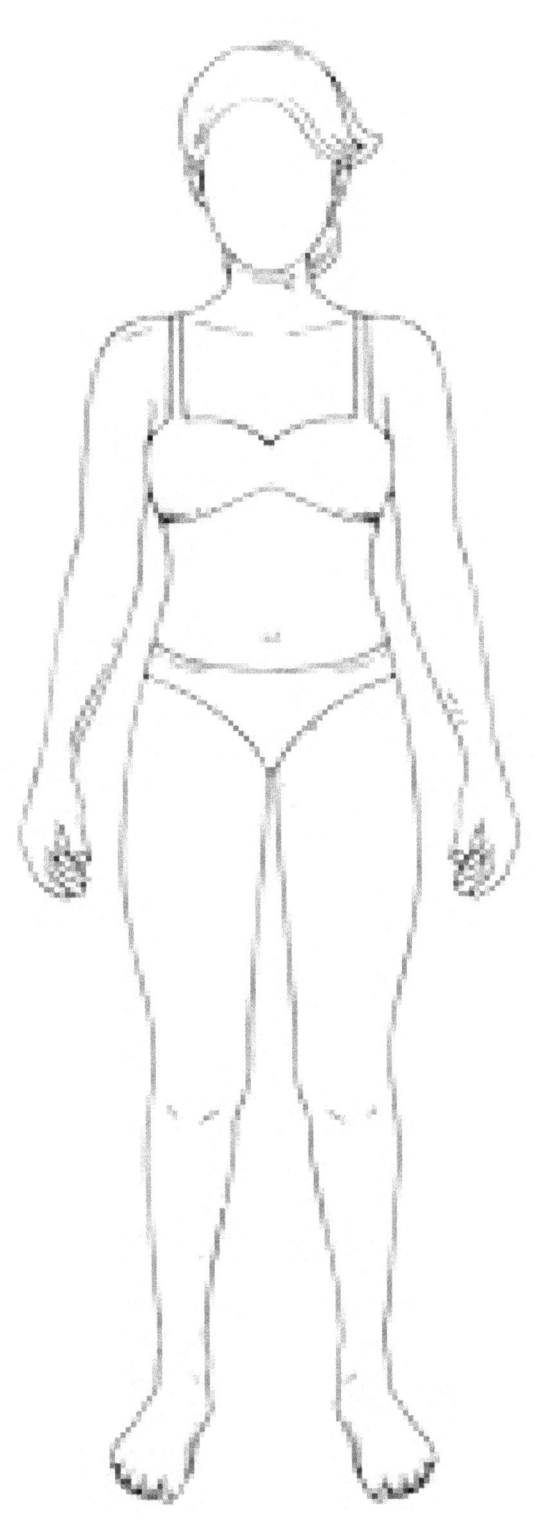

/5

She lives in the 20's

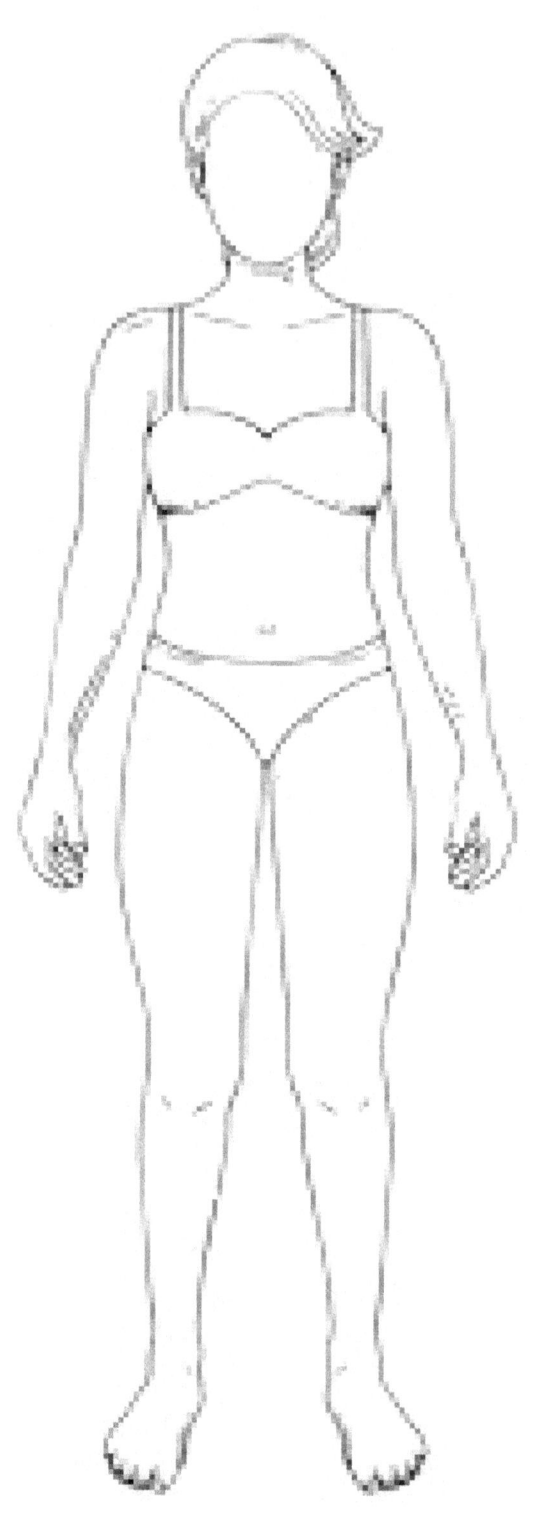

/5

She is the best student in her class

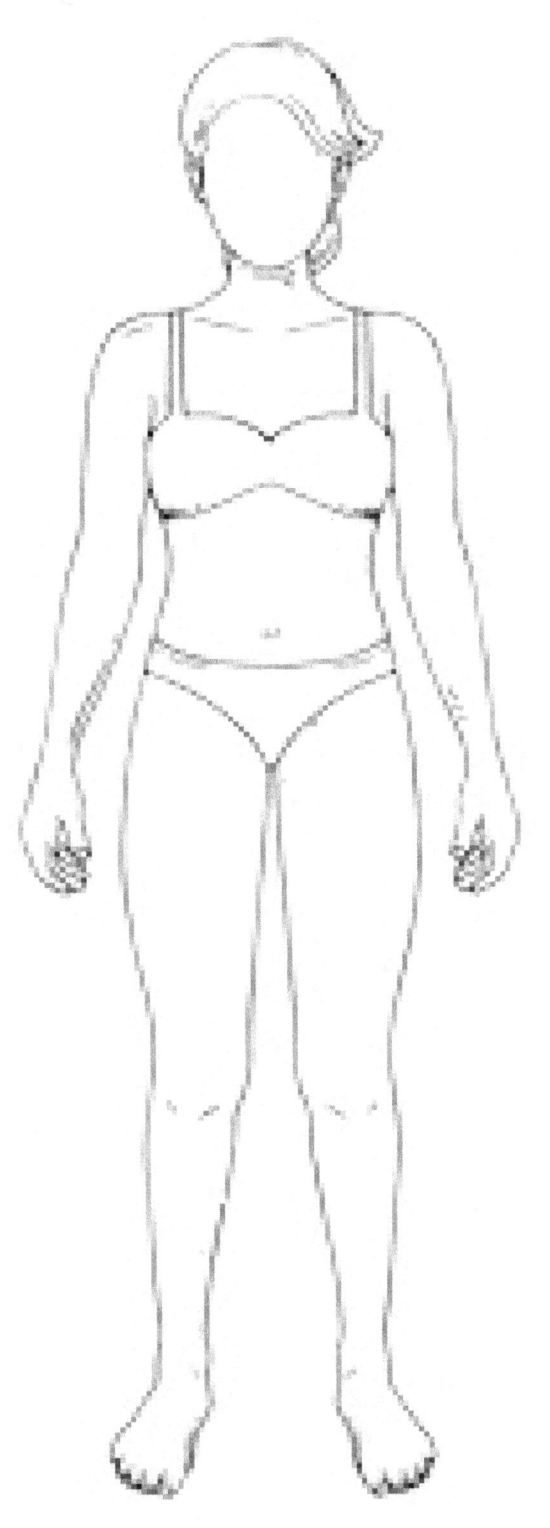

/5

She hates dark colors

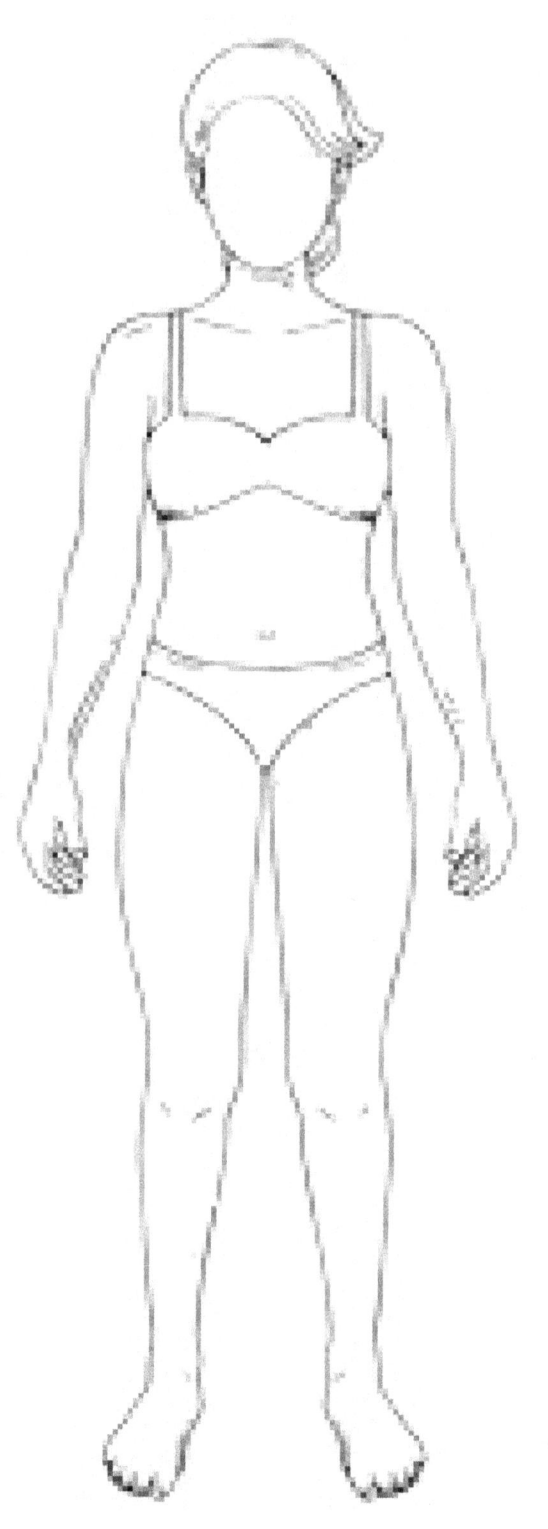

/5

She was late

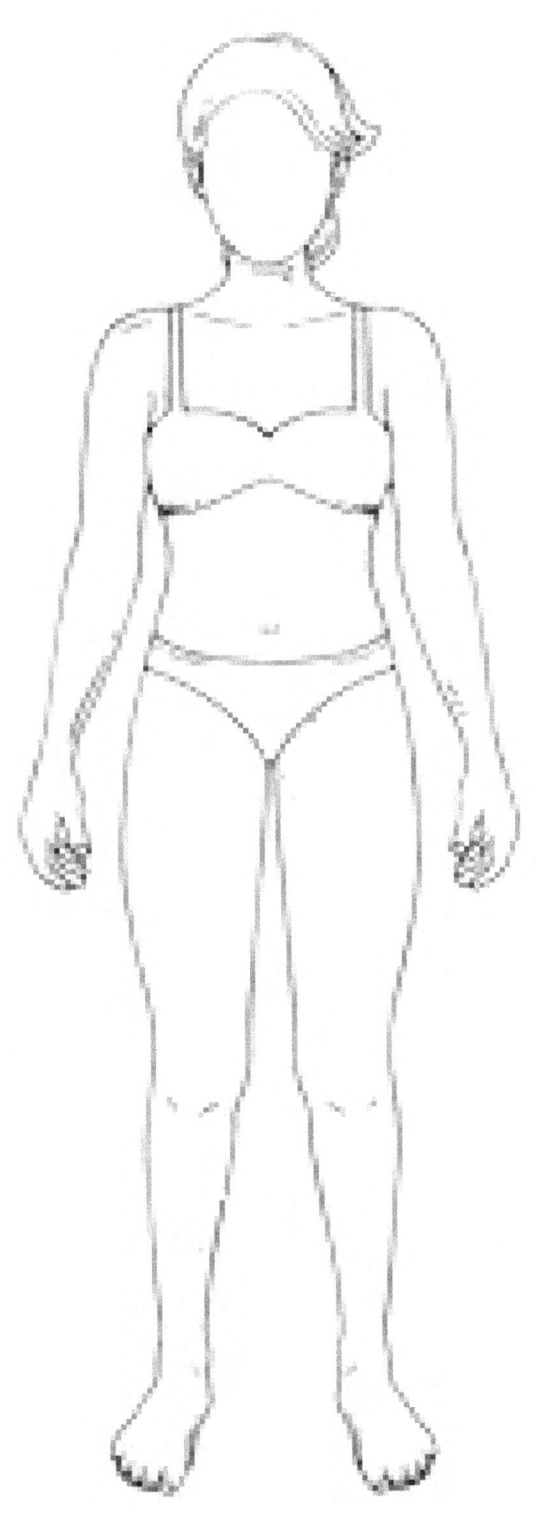

/5

She is learning how to cook

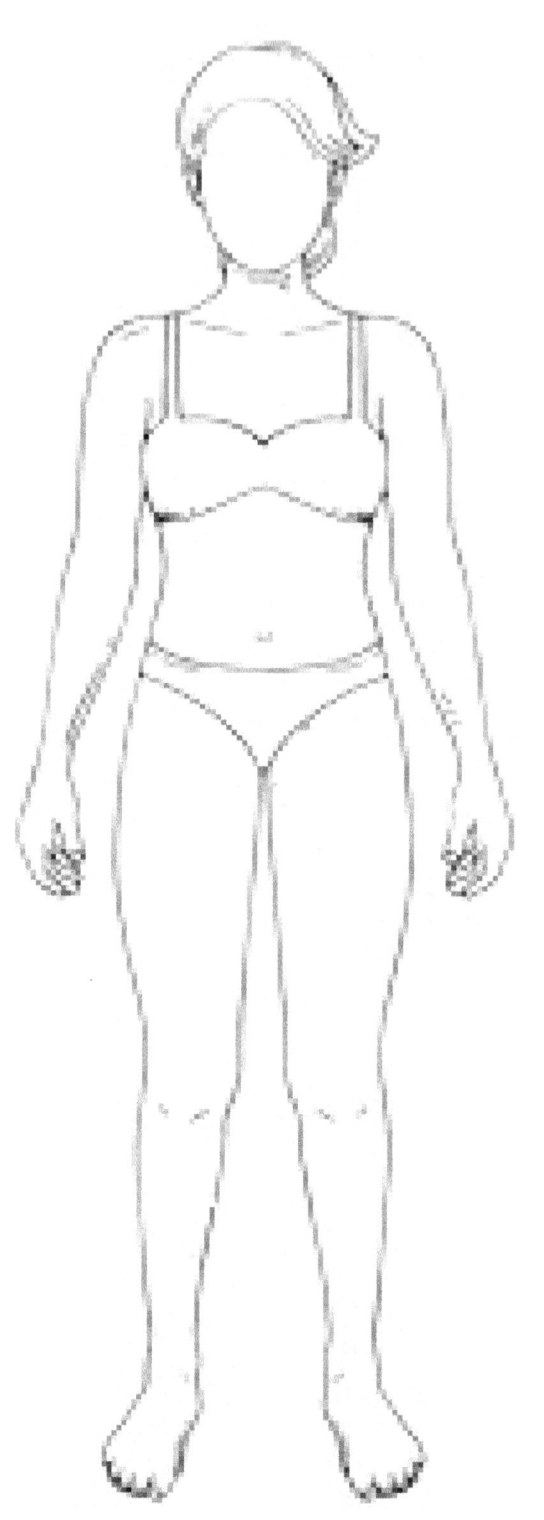

/5

She is the main character in a play

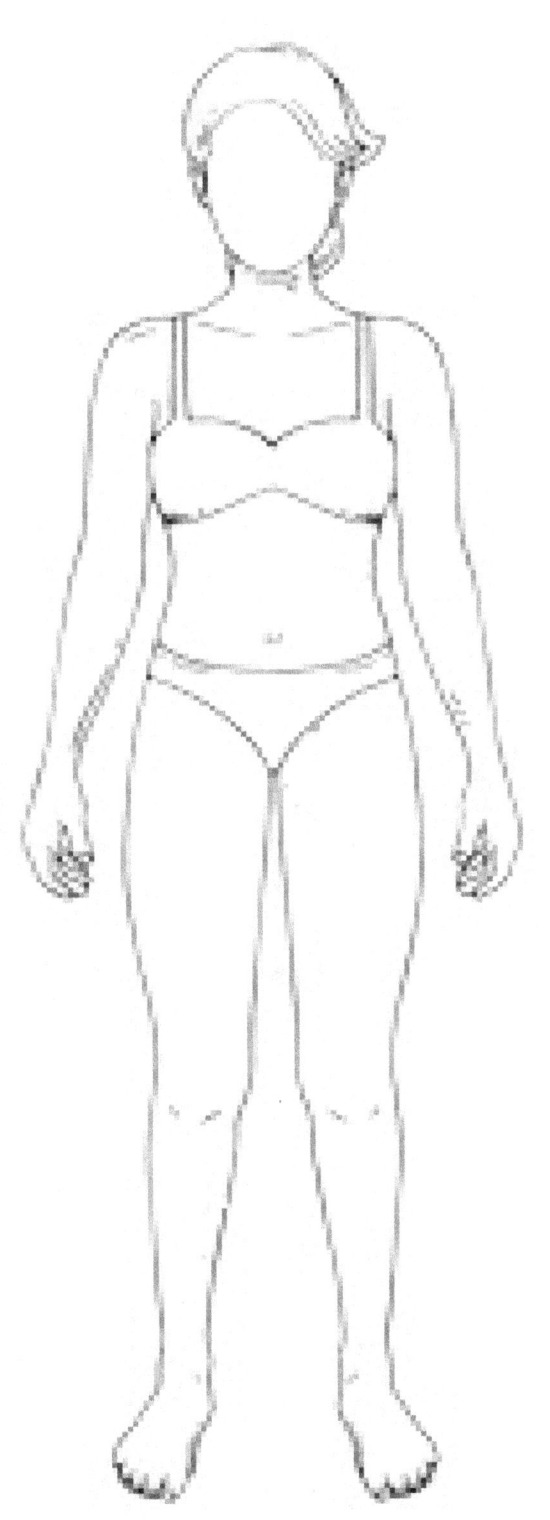

/5

She loves our planet

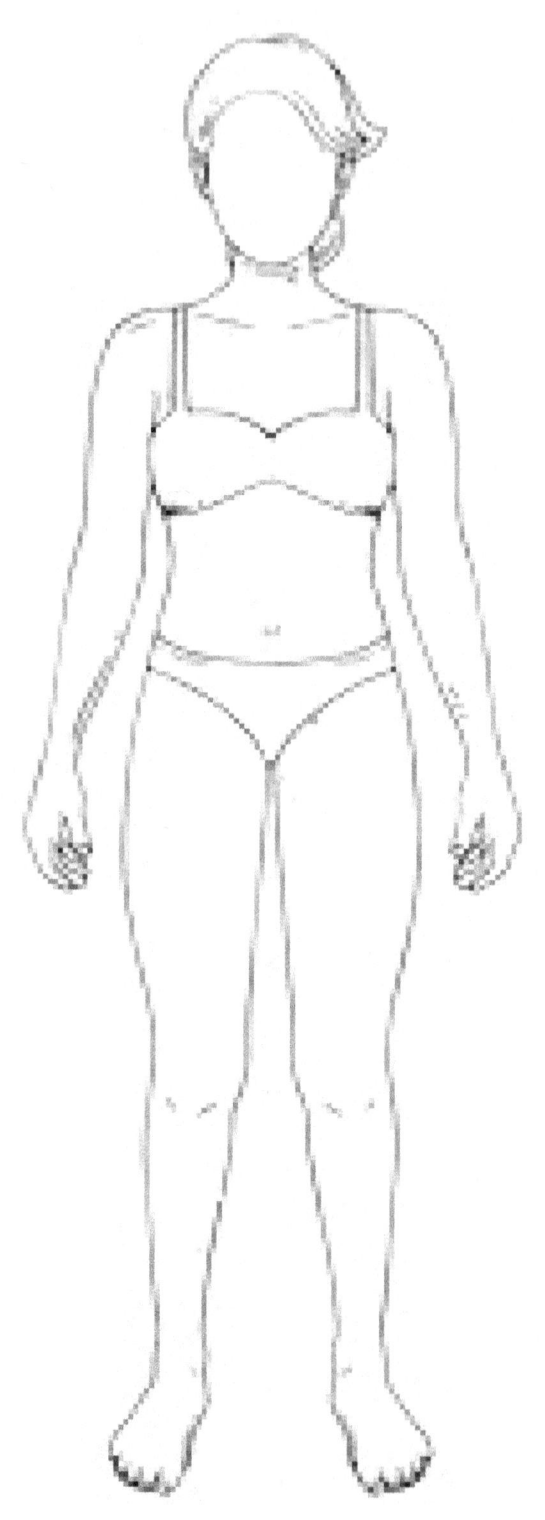

/5

She's from another planet

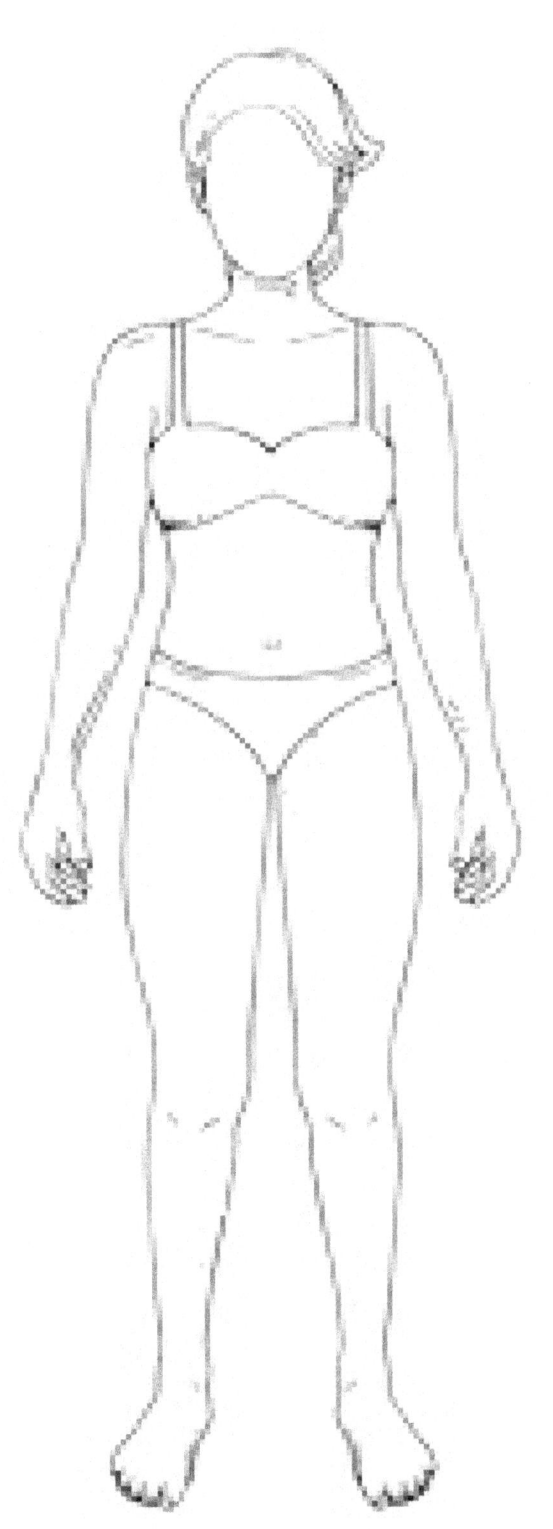

/5

Outside it's -20 C°

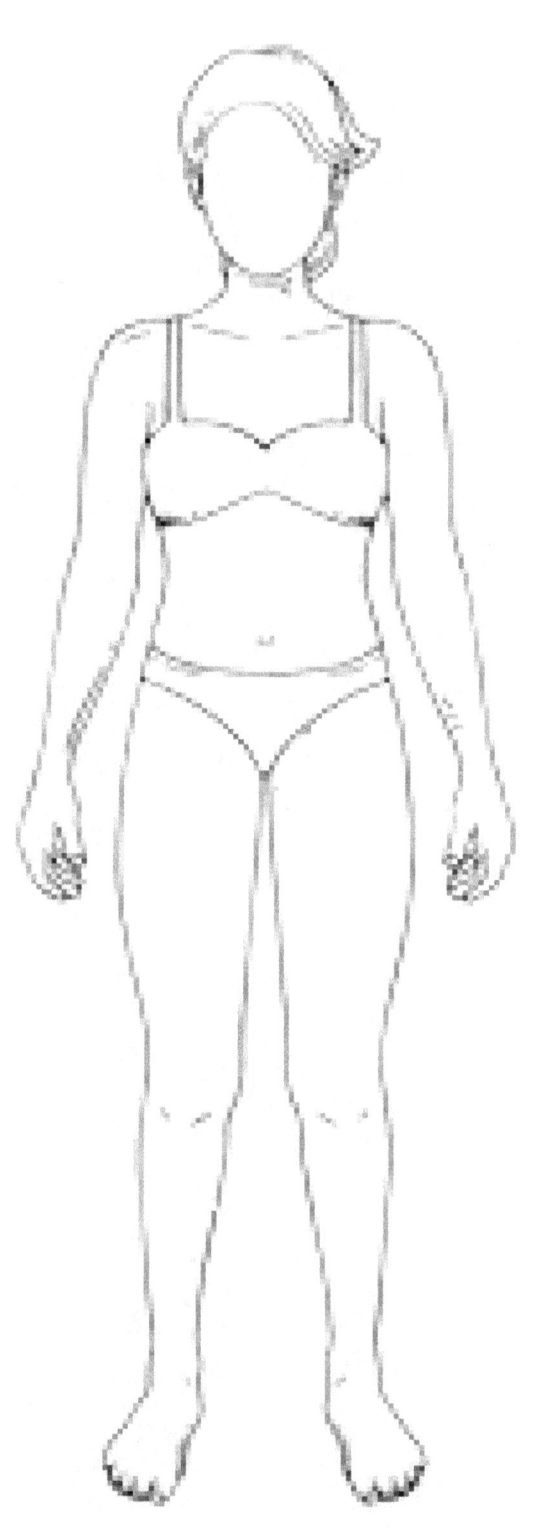

She is the queen of the prom

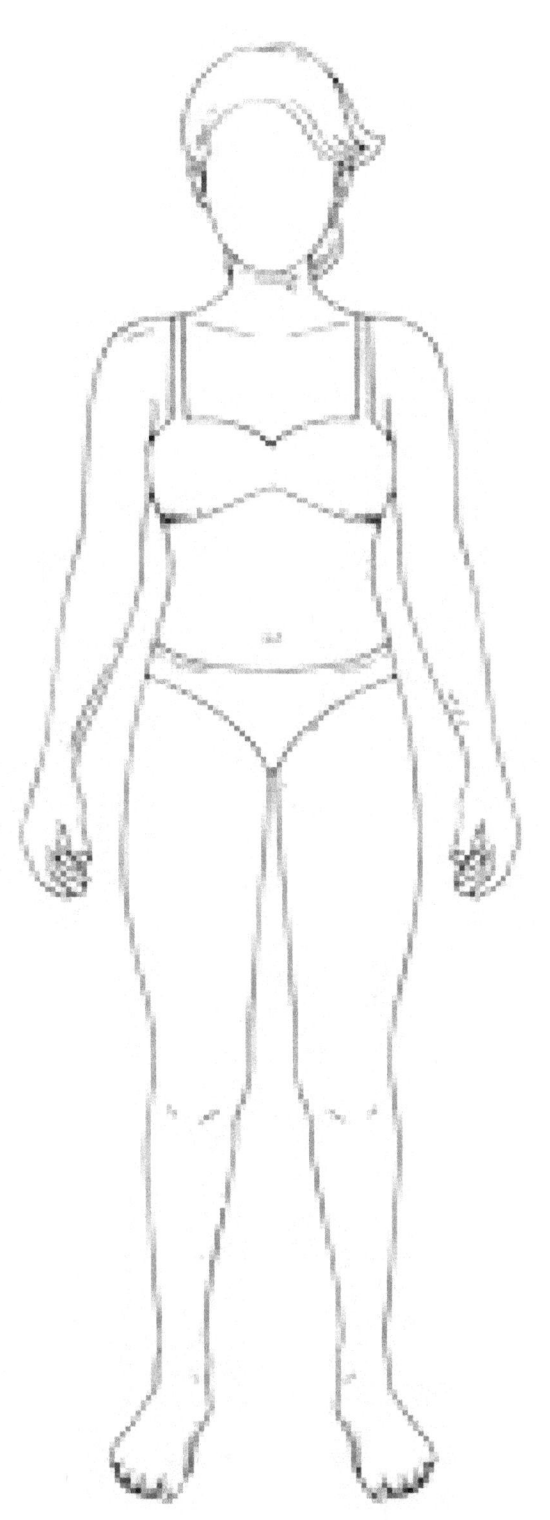

/5

She loves danger

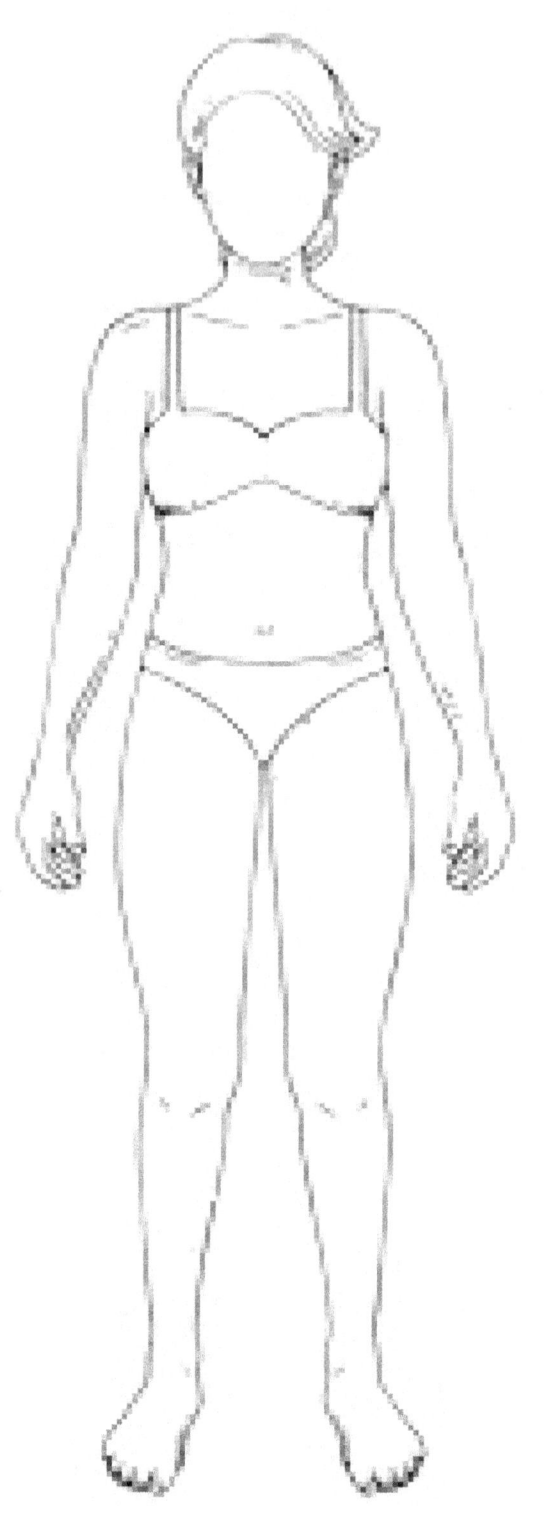

/5

She is a fashion designer

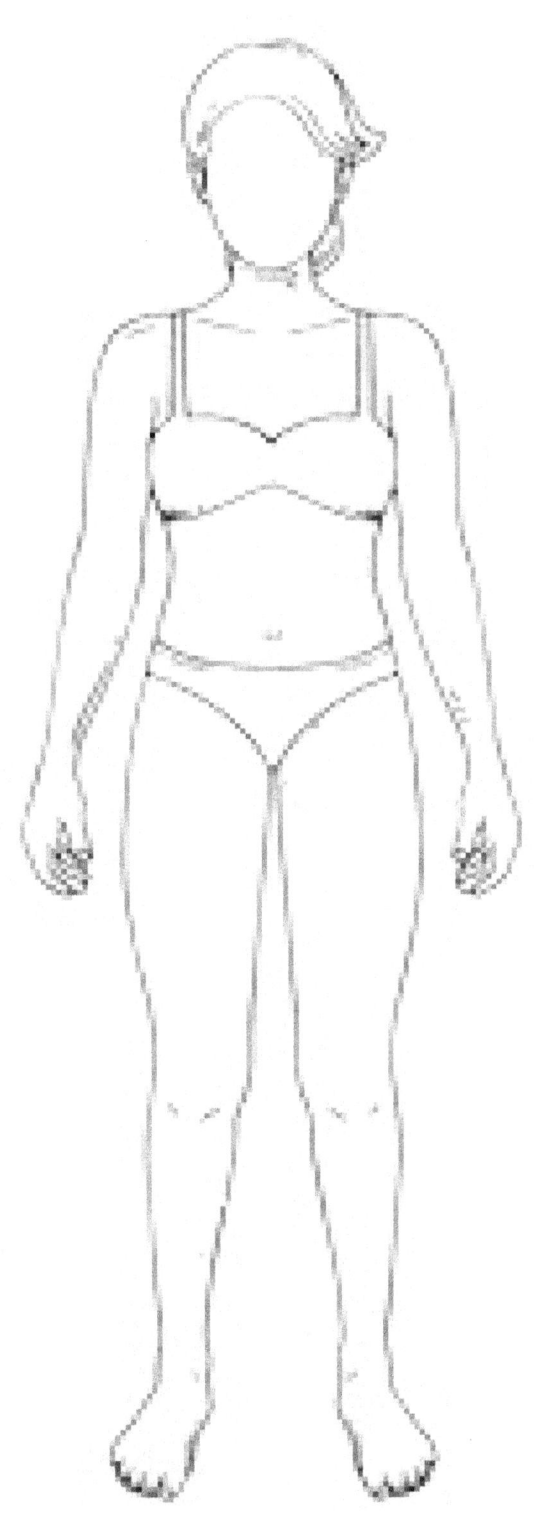

/5

She lives with 7 cats

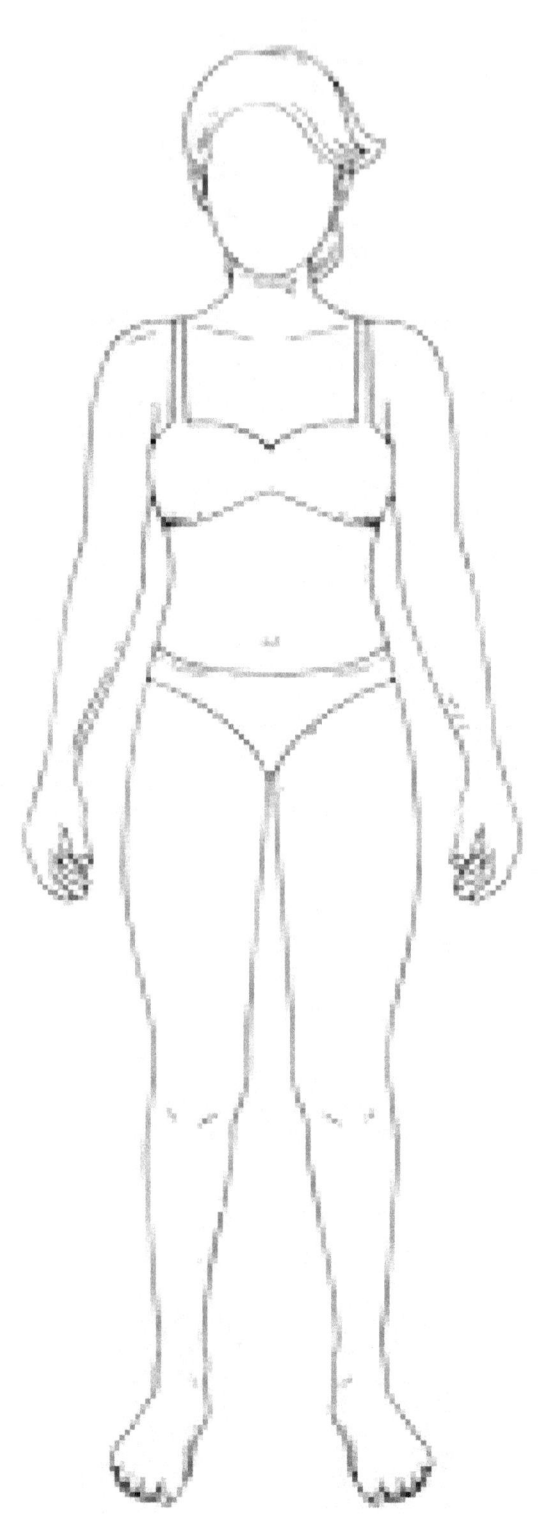

/5

She's the heroine of the city

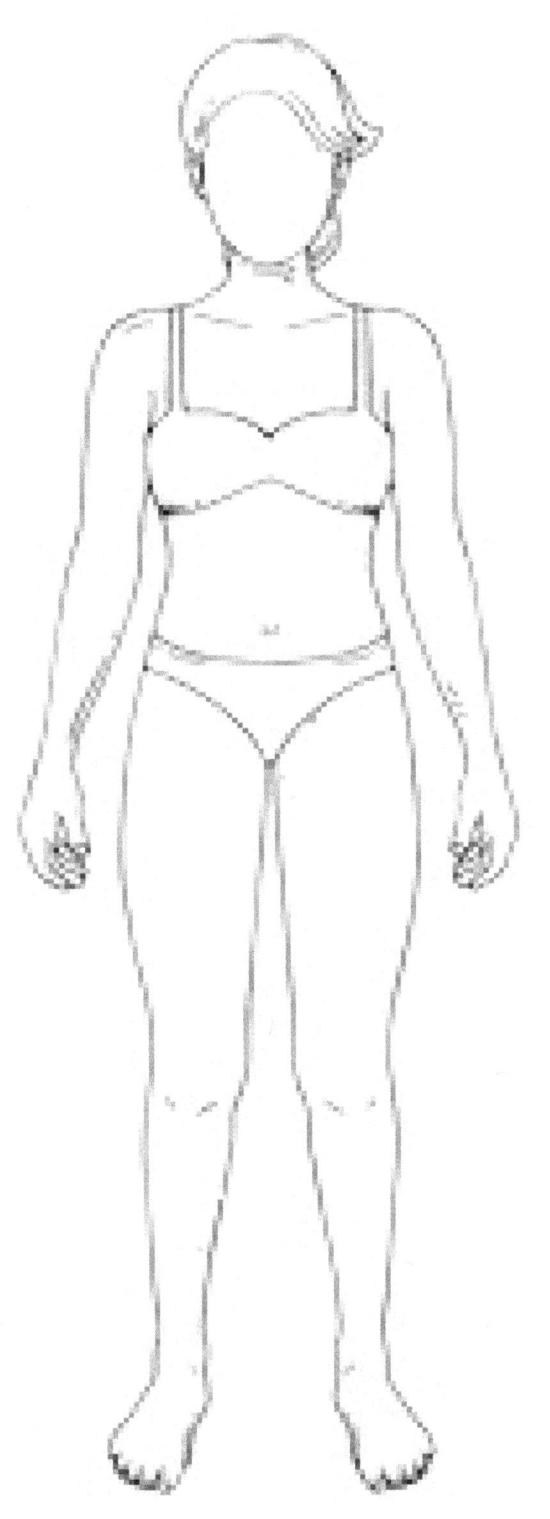

/5

She's the CEO of a bank

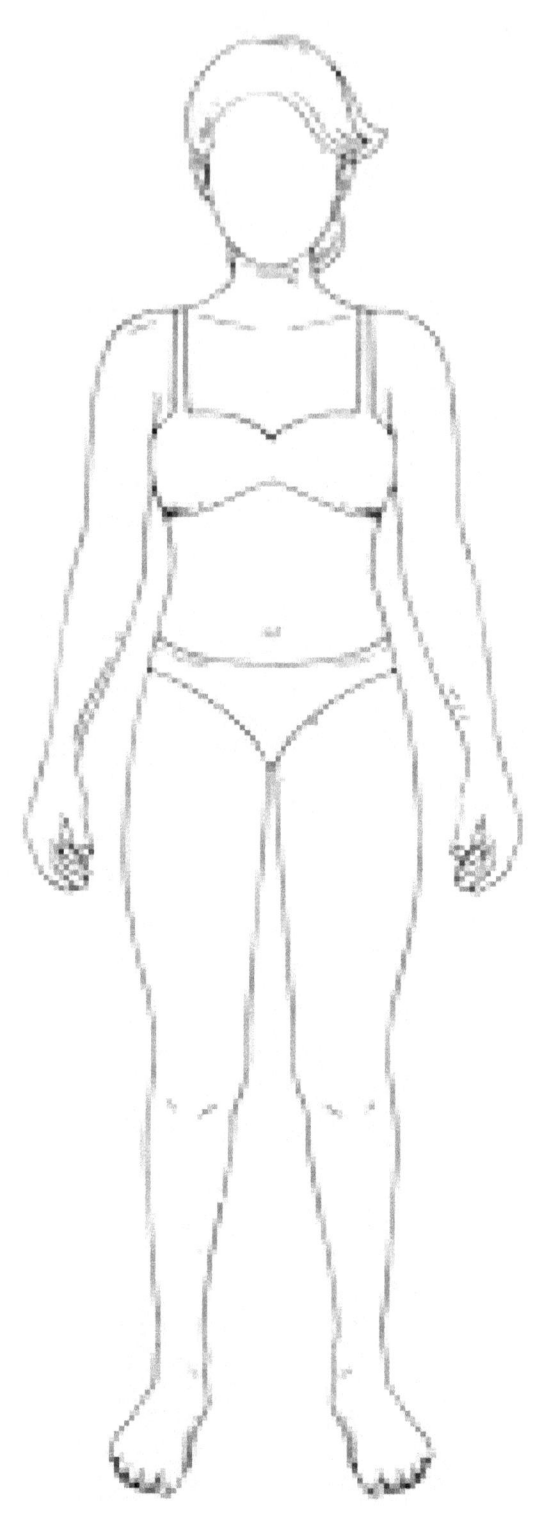

/5

It's the 31 of October

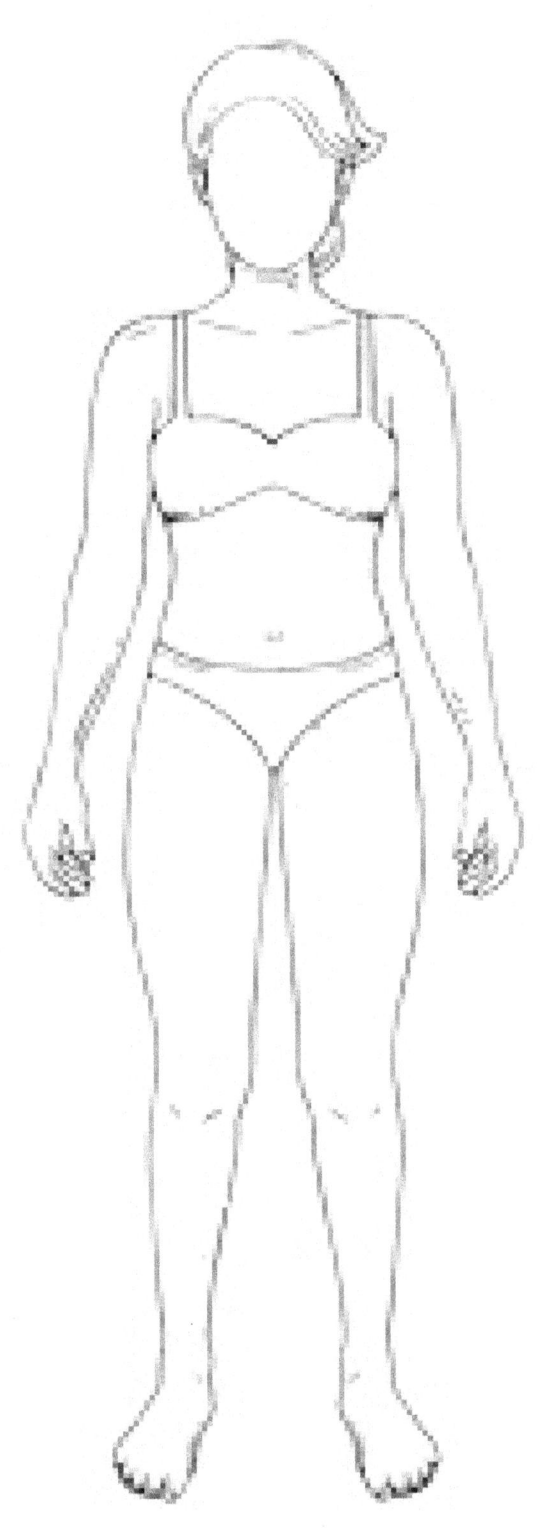

/5

She is sick

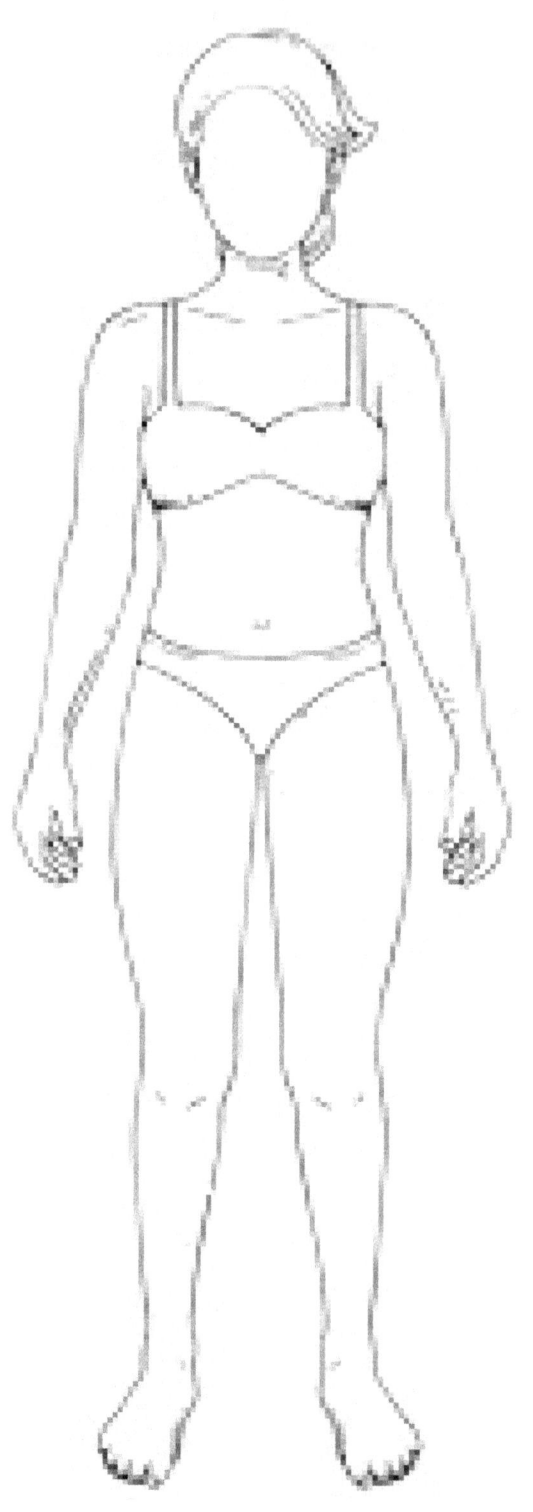

/5

She lives in the woods

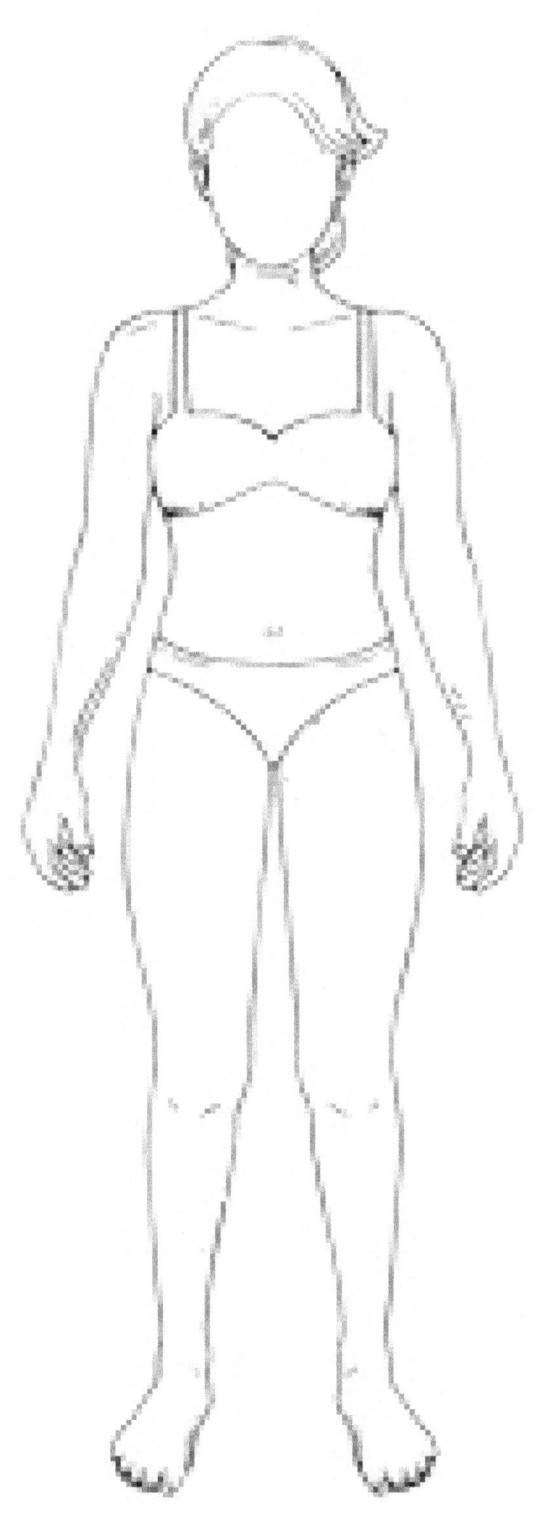

/5

She's the soul of the party

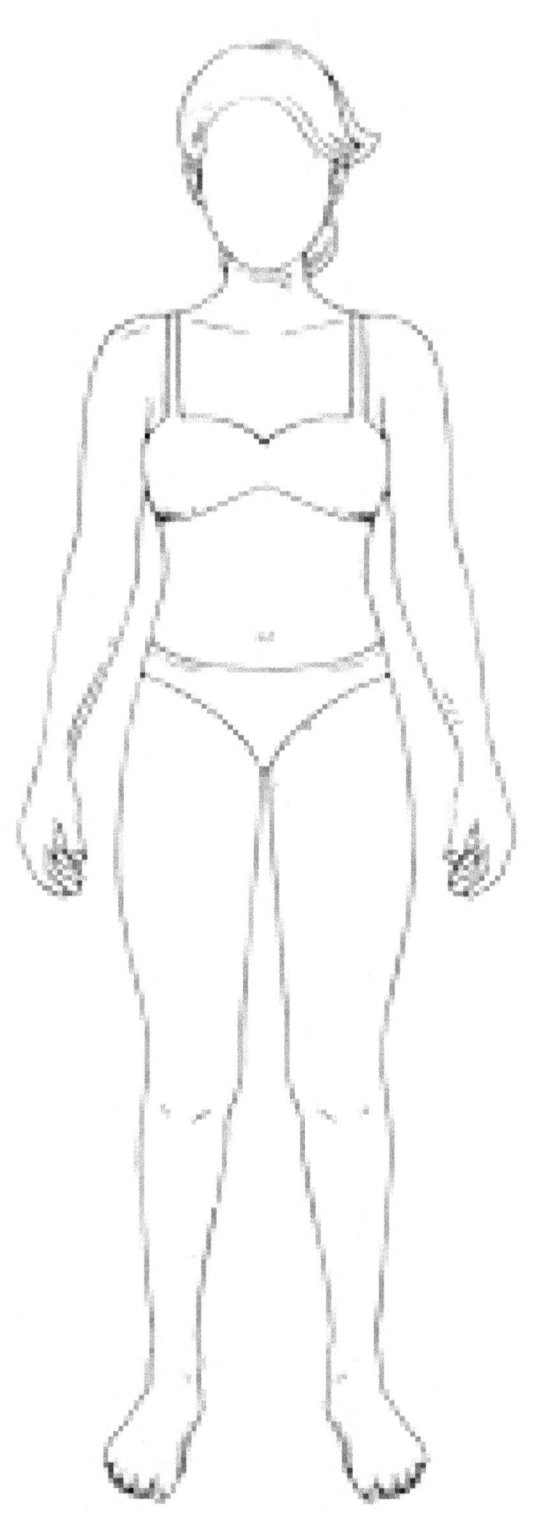

/5

She's someone to be afraid of

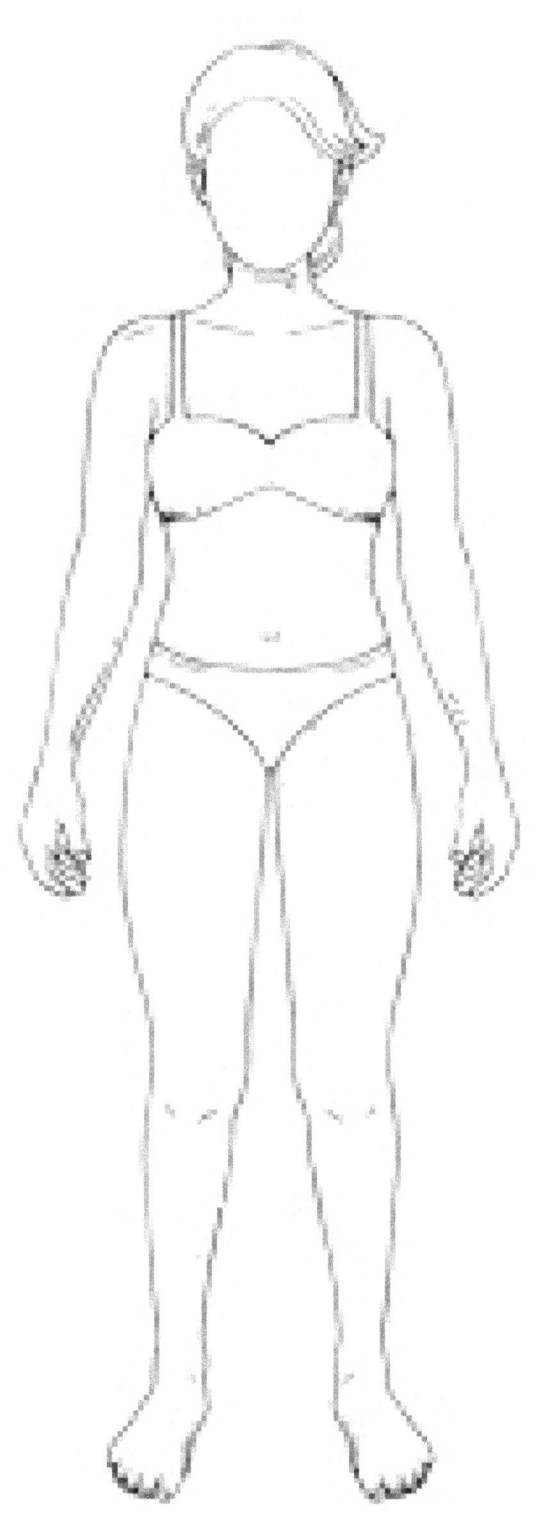

/5

She only eats junk food

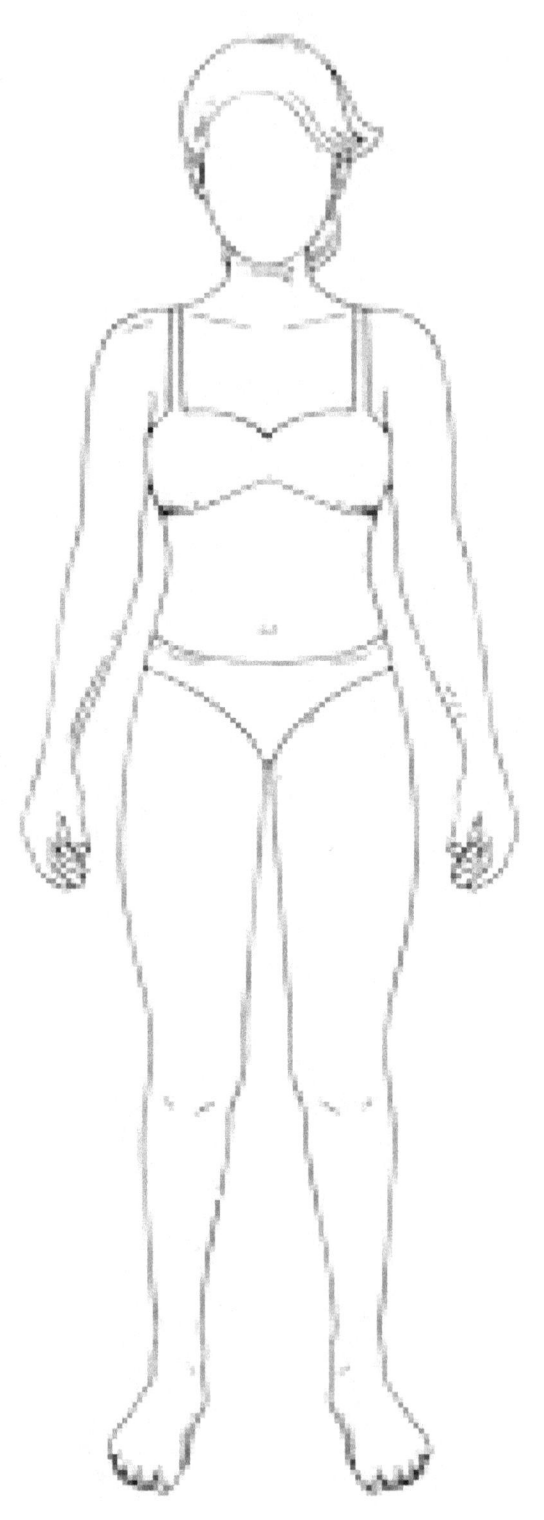

/5

She wants to be misterious

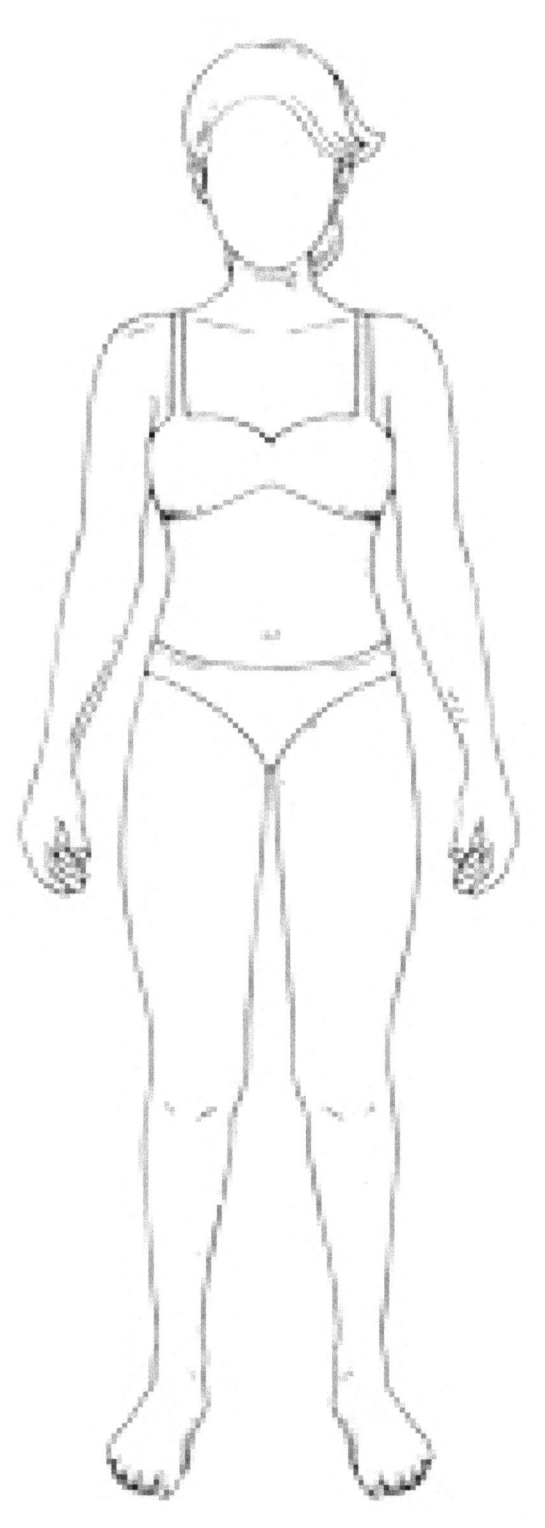

/5

She lives in a dangerous country

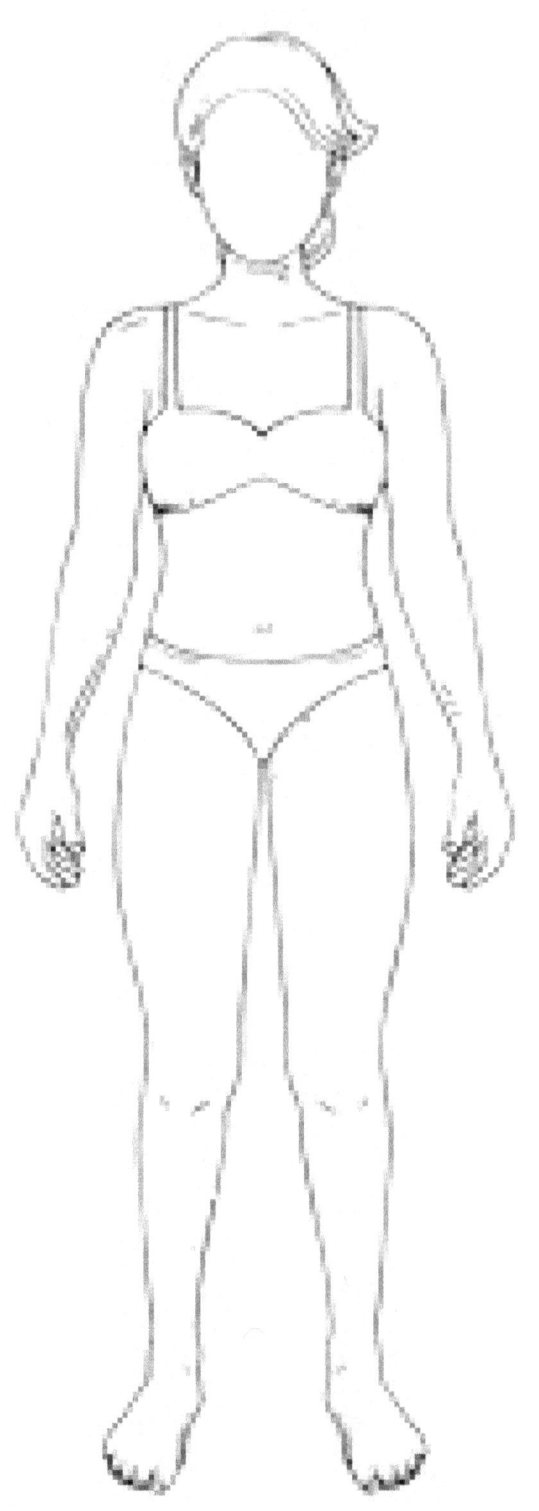

/5

She reads a lot of books

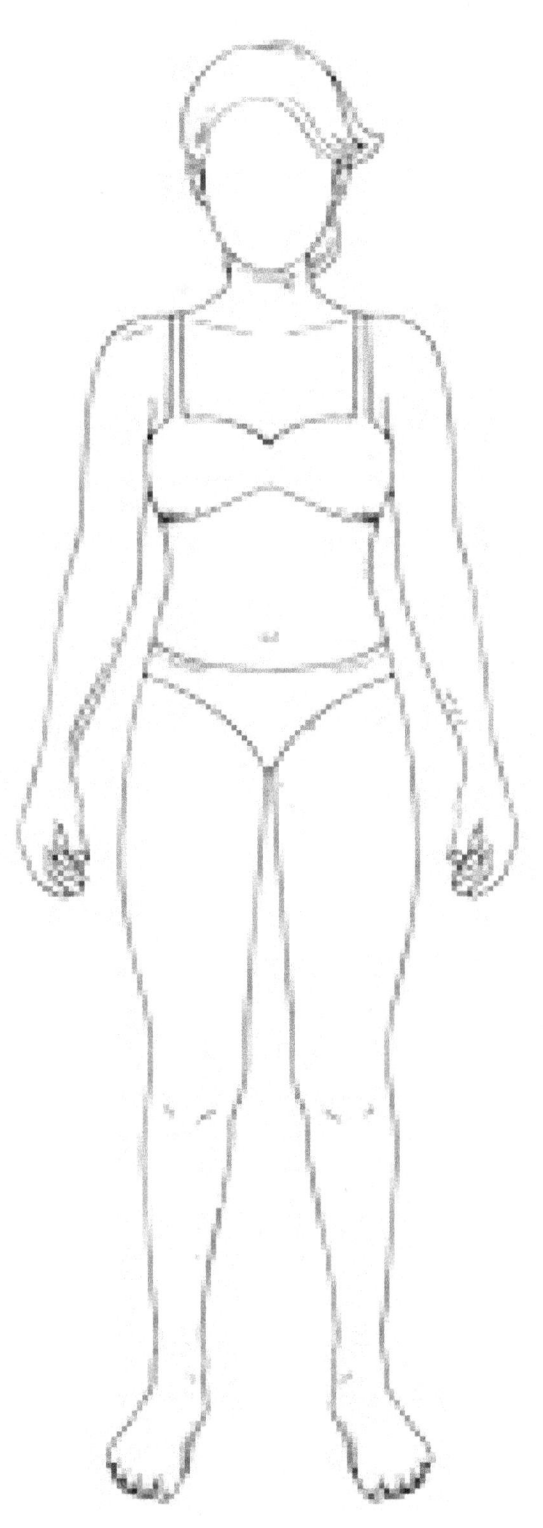

/5

She's the laziest person alive

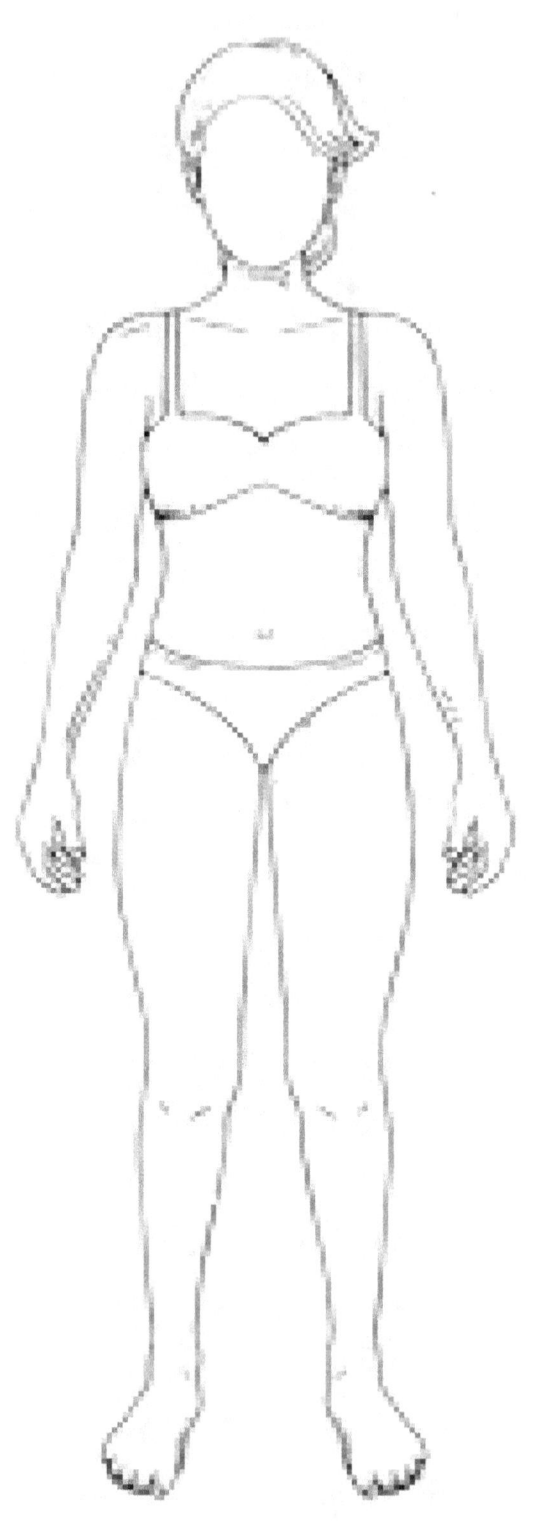

/5

Everybody fall in love with her

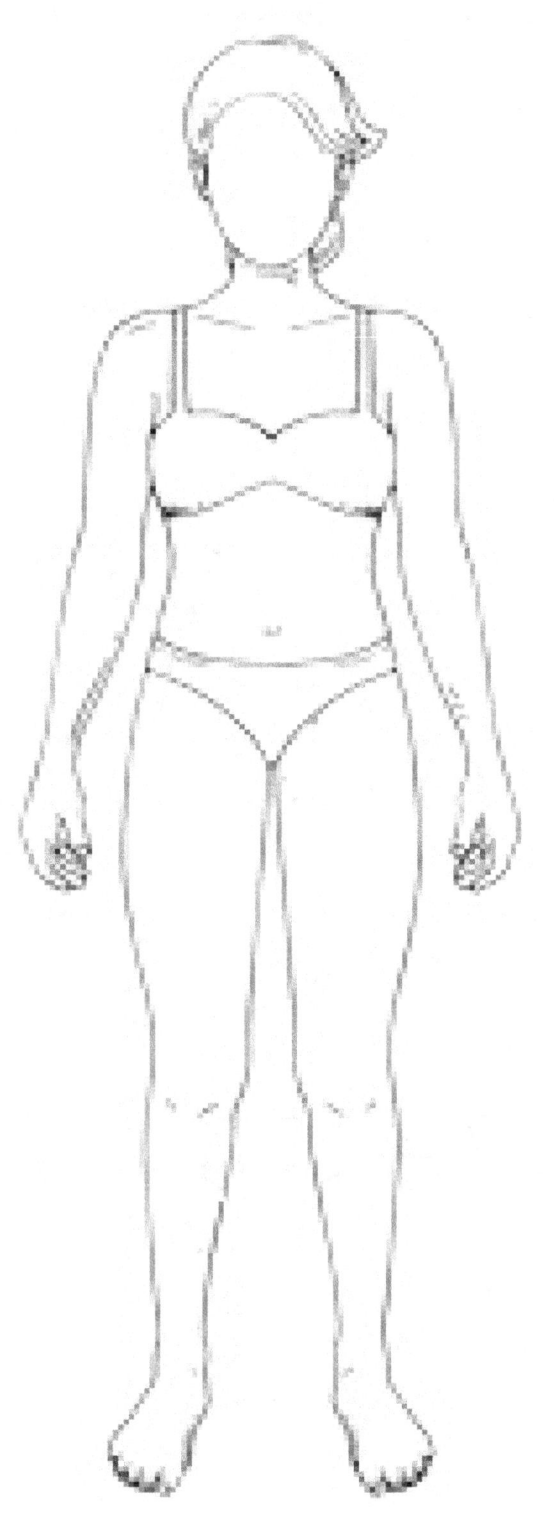

/5

Final Results:

/155

CONGRATULATIONS!

www.ingramcontent.com/pod-product-compliance
Lightning Source LLC
Chambersburg PA
CBHW081021240526
45471CB00018B/3927